Acer Aspire 5 S User Guide

A Complete Guide to Get You Started

Ella Brown

Contents

Copyright © 2021 Ella Brown 2

INTRODUCTION...1

Know Your Device 2

CAUTION!..2

Basic things you need to know about your computer Device: 3

    Turning OFF your computer..3

    To put your device on a sleep mode:..4

Cleaning and servicing 4

Know Your Computer Device 5

    Screen view 5

    Icon Item Description...5

    KEYBOARD VIEW 6

    Icon Item Description...6

    RIGHT VIEW..7

    Icon Item Description...7

    LEFT VIEW 8

    Icon Item Description...8

    Rear View 9

    Icon Item Description...9

    Base View..9

    Icon Item Description...10

USING THE KEYBOARD 10

USING THE PRECISION TOUCHPAD..11

Using the Keyboard – 15 HotKeys to activate hotkeys 12

CONNECTING TO THE INTERNET..13

Connecting to a wireless network..14

Connecting to the internet 15

Connecting with a cable Built-in network feature 17

Connecting to a cellular network..18

    BLUELIGHT SHIELD 18

SECURING YOUR COMPUTER..19

Using a computer security lock...20

Entering passwords...21

BIOS UTILITY...22

Boot sequence 22

Setting passwords 22

POWER MANAGEMENT 23

    Saving Power Disable Fast startup...................................23

BATTERY PACK...25

    Battery characteristics 25

    Charging the battery 25

    Conditioning a new battery pack 26

    Optimizing battery life 27

    Checking the battery level 28

    Battery Low warning 28

TRAVELLING WITH YOUR COMPUTER....................................29

    Disconnecting from the desktop.......................................29

    Moving around...30

    Preparing the computer..30

What to bring to meetings 31

Taking the computer home 31

Preparing the computer 32

Special considerations 32

Setting up a home office 33

Ports and connectors 34

UNIVERSAL SERIAL BUS (USB) 34

Inserting an SD Card 35

SD, SDHC, and SDXC cards 36

VIDEO AND AUDIO CONNECTORS 36

Headphones and microphone 37

HDMI 37

BIOS UTILITY 39

Boot sequence 39

Setting passwords 39

POWER MANAGEMENT 40

Saving Power Disable Fast startup 40

BATTERY PACK 42

Battery characteristics 42

Charging the battery 42

Conditioning a new battery pack 42

Optimizing battery life 44

Checking the battery level 45

Battery Low warning 45

The power outlet or AC adapter is not available? 45

TRAVELLING WITH YOUR COMPUTER..46

Disconnecting from the desktop..46

Moving around 46

INTRODUCTION

The Acer aspire 5 slim laptop comes in multiple colors and with powerful processors and graphics. It gives its users various choices to get the most of its newest features which ranges from fast Wi-Fi, plenty of storage to the latest connectivity, fantastic data transfer speed with USB 5Gbps(2 units), Type A Ports which could be used for offline charging with a total of four (4) USB ports in all.

This book is a guide to help you optimize the use of your Acer Aspire 5 slim laptop device. Here, we have compilation of set of guides to help you get started with the setting up of your computer device and how to use all of the latest features that comes along with it.

In this guide, you will be introduced to the basic features of your device and their functionalities and its maintenance for optimum utility.

Know Your Device

CAUTION!

• Ensure the use of the adapter provided along with your device or an Acer approved adapter to power it.

• Do not place the device too close to source of intense heat or direct sunlight.

• Magnetic fields could cause damage to your device.

• Rain, moisture, water spillage or any liquid on your device could cause severe damage to it.

• Avoid any action that may subject your device to heavy shock or vibration.

• Clean your computer always to get rid of dust or dirt from your device.

• Do not place objects (heavy) on your device.

• Do not place the power cord where it could be stepped on. Always make sure it is not on the walk way.

• Pull out the plug and not the cord during unplugging.

• When using an extension cord, ensure the total ampere and current ratings of the extension equipment do not exceed that of the cord.

Basic things you need to know about your computer Device:

Turning OFF your computer: Do one of the following:

• Using the Windows shutdown command, select the Windows Start button > Power and then, select Shut down. or

• Right-click on the Window's Start button and do either of the following:

Select Shut down: If you need to power down the computer completely.

Select sign-out: if you only need to short down but don't want to completely switch-off your device, you can also put it on a Sleep mode.

To put your device on a sleep mode:
• select the power button > sleep hotkey > Windows key or Start button > Power > Sleep.

• Select the Start button > sign out or shut-down > Sleep

Cleaning and servicing

The following steps should be taken before cleaning the computer:

1. Shut down the computer.

2. Disconnect the device from the adapter.

3. Use a very soft and fairly moist material to do the cleaning. Avoid the use of liquid or aerosol to clean.

If your computer device is not functioning properly or if you notice any visible damage, then contact the nearest authorized Acer computer servicing center.

Know Your Computer Device

Now that your computer is fully set-up, read ahead and get to know more about your new Acer Aspire computer device.

Screen view

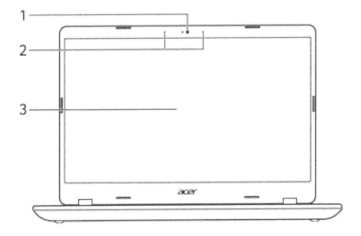

Icon Item Description

1 **Web camera** (Webcam) this is used for video communication: when the webcam is active, there will be an indication from a light flash next to the webcam.

2 **Microphone** (An Internal digital microphone) used to record voice or sound.

3 this is the **Visual display unit** (VDU). It displays the computer out-put.

KEYBOARD VIEW

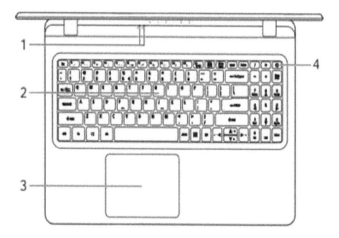

Icon Item Description

1 the **Power indicator**: Indicates the device's power status. It indicates when the battery is in charging mode, fully charged or in AC mode.

2 **Keyboard:** this is used For inputting data into your computer device.

. 3 **Touchpad**: this is a Touch-sensitive pointing device. To perform a "Left click", press the touchpad surface firmly. And for a right-click, press the lower-right corner of the icon down.

4 **Power button**: this is used to turn ON or OFF the computer.

RIGHT VIEW

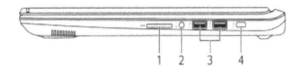

Icon Item Description

1 **card reader**: this is an impute system which Accepts a Secure Digital (SD, SDXC or SDHC) card.

2 **Headset/ speaker jack**: this is used to Connects to audio devices like headphones or speakers.

3 **USB ports**: this is used to Connects USB devices.

4 **USB Type-C ports**: this is used to Connects USB devices that are of the USB Type-C connector.

LEFT VIEW

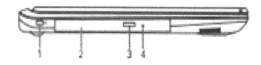

Icon Item Description

1 **Kensington lock slot**: this Connected to a security lock that is kensinton compatible.

2 **Optical drive:** this is an internal drive that accepts CDs or DVDs.

3 **Eject button**: this is used to Ejects optical disk from the optical drive.

4 **Emergency eject hole:** it is used to Ejects the optical drive tray. It serves as an alternative eject mechanism when the computer is turned off. It involves the use of a straight paper clip to eject the drive tray.

Rear View

Icon Item Description

1 **DC-in jack**: this is where the AC adapter is connected to.

2 **HDMI port**: here is where high-definition digital video are connected to.

3 **Ethernet (RJ-45) port**: it is used to Connect to Ethernet based network.

Base View

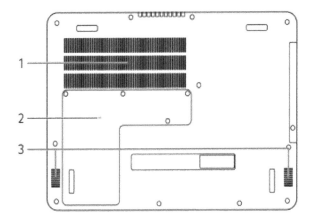

Icon Item Description

1. **Ventilation and cooling fan**: this serves as an outlet for heat or hot air and inlets for cool air. It is a cooling system for the computer. The openings must not be obstructed else it may lead to overheating of the computer system.

2 **Battery reset pinhole**: this pinhole is a stimulator for removing and reinstalling the battery.

3 **Speakers**: for sound delivery.

USING THE KEYBOARD

The keyboard has a numeric keypad, full-sized keys, separate cursor, special keys and hotkeys, lock, and Windows.

Lock keys: You can use the lock keys in your keyboard to turn keyboard functions on and off.

Special keys: There are keys in your computer's keyboard that activate special functions. The function of every key is vividly marked with an icon.

Lock Key Description Caps Lock: All alphabetic characters inserted are in uppercase when caps lock is on.

Num Lock (Numeric Lock): The keypad is in numeric mode when Num Lock is on. The keys function as a calculator (complete with the arithmetic operations *, +, -, and /). When you need to do a lot of numeric data entry, simply use this mode.

Scr Lk (Scroll Lock): As long as the screen lock is on, the screen will certainly move up or down; but only when you hit the up or down arrow keys respectively. Scroll Lock does not apply with a few applications. The computer will be in sleep mode if you use the icon function description sleep.

Windows key can return to the Start screen or even the last open application if you press it alone.

Application Key – Clicking the right mouse button is basically the same effect with this key.

USING THE PRECISION TOUCHPAD

The arrow or cursor on the screen is controlled by the touchpad. The cursor will follow the movement as you slide your finger across the touchpad. The Precision Tocuhpad (PTP) is designed to offer a smooth, uniform, and accurate touchpad experience. A lot of applications support precision touchpad gestures that make use of one Airplane mode turns off or on the computer's network devices. The screen brightness is decreased or increased if you use the brightness key.

Using the Keyboard – 15 HotKeys to activate hotkeys

- Long-press the Fn Key, then hit the other key in the hotkey combination.
- The Display toggle switches is meant to display output amidst the display screen. To save power, simply use the Display key to turn off the display screen backlight. Touch any key to return.
- The built-in touchpad can be turned on or off as long as you toggle the keyboard. The keyboard backlight can be turned on or off as long as you toggle the keyboard backlight. Function varies depending on configuration.
- The speakers can be turned on or off if you toggle the speaker.
- The sound volume is decreased or even increasednd that it is necessary to check your devices owner's manual to determine how to turn on its Bluetooth adapter.

- Choose the device you intend to pair from the list of discovered devices.

- Once you pair, you can choose to enter a code displaying on the screen. This code will help in the connection process.

CONNECTING TO THE INTERNET

This chapter is basically about the kinds of connections and the basic steps in getting connected to the internet.

As long as you have the built-in network features, you can easily connect your computer to the internet. But first and foremost, you will need to sign up for internet services to connect to the internet from home. You can sign up from an ISP (internet service provider). The internet service provider is like a cable company or phone company that will come to your home or workplace to set up internet service.

A small box, a modem, and a router will be installed by the ISP. These features will let you to connect to the internet.

Connecting to a wireless network

Connecting to a wireless network (LAN or WLAN) will help to link two or more computers without using wires. Remember, the LAN or WLAN are both wireless local area networks. When you connect to WLAN, you can access the internet. Besides, you can share files to other devices. Your computer's wireless connection is turned on by default and Windows will detect and show a list of available networks during setup. Before you insert the password, simply choose your network.

An airplane mode hotkey is usually featured by the Acer notebook computers. This airplane mode hotkey turns the network connection off or on. You can turn your wireless network on or off or even control what is shared over the network by using the network management options. Keep in mind that it is prohibited to use wireless devices in an aircraft, especially when it is flying. Before you board an aircraft and during takeoff, you must switch off all wireless devices. If you do not switch it off, then you can cause danger to the operation of the aircraft, disrupt communications, and even commit a crime. You can only turn on your computer's wireless devices when you are informed by the cabin crew it is safe to do so.

Connecting to the internet

Please follow the steps below if you want to connect to a wireless network;

- First and foremost, make sure you are in possession of the access point or wireless router and also the current internet connection through the ISP of your preferred option. Then, make a note of the wireless password and name. Make sure you have the wireless network's name if you are trying to connect to a public network like a coffee shop.

- In the notification area, simply click Network icon

- It will display all available wireless networks. Simply choose the specific wireless network you intend to use

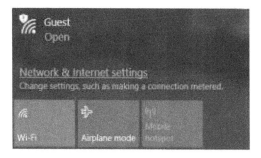

- Choose the Connect button when you choose a wireless network

- Insert the network's password, if required.

Connecting with a cable Built-in network feature

Let us assume your computer has a network port, simply plug one end of a network cable into the network port on your computer. Afterwards, plug the other end into a port on your router. Finally, you should be ready to get online.

Connecting to a cellular network

Let us assume your computer has a SIM slot, you can use the cellular phone network to connect to the internet. Before this can be done, you must be in possession of a compatible SIM card and a data contract with your cellular provider. For more information on using a cellular network to connect to the internet, simply contact your cellular provider.

BLUELIGHT SHIELD

Once you enable the blue light shield, you can reduce the blue-light emissions from the screen to safeguard your eyes. Search for 'Quick Access' in the Start menu to configure the Bluelight shield. From here, you can choose from four different modes to fit your requirements and also toggle Bluelight shield on or off.

1. Low Reduction decreases blue light emission from the LED backlit screen by 10 percent to 25 percent for basic protection

2. Medium reduction decreases blue light emission from the LED backlit screen by 26 percent to 45 percent to safeguard your eyes.

3. High Reduction decreases blue light emission from the LED backlit screen by 46 percent to 65 percent for maximum protection.

4. Long Hour Mode professionally tuned to decrease eye strain over a long period.

SECURING YOUR COMPUTER

Since your computer is a valuable investment, you need to take care of it. Learn the basic methods of safeguarding your computer. The hardware and software locks, that is, the security notch and passwords are included in the security features.

Using a computer security lock

A computer security slot is always inside a computer for a security lock. Wrap a computer security lock cable around a fixed object like a handle of a locked drawer or a table. Before you turn the key to secure the lock, simply insert the lock into the notch. There are also some available keyless models. You can protect your computer from unauthorized access if you use the passwords. Several different levels of protection for your data and computer are created by setting these passwords;

- Supervisor password hinders unauthorized entry into the BIOS utility. You can gain access to the BIOS utility by entering the password.
- Your computer is secured against unauthorized use by the user password. Use the password checkpoints on boot-up to combine the use of this password. Then, resume from hibernation for maximum security.

- Your computer is secured against unauthorized use by the password on boot. Use the password checkpoints on boot-up to combine the use of this password. Then, resume from hibernation for maximum security.

Entering passwords

A password prompt displays in the center of the display screen when a password is set.

- A prompt displays when you insert the BIOS utility, but only when the supervisor password is set.
- Insert the supervisor password and hit the Enter button to access the BIOS utility. A warning message appears when you insert the password incorrectly. Try again and hit the Enter button.
- A prompt appears at boot-up when the User password is set and the password on boot parameter is enabled.
- Insert the User password and hit the Enter button to use the computer. . A warning message appears when you insert the password incorrectly. Try again and hit the Enter button.

BIOS UTILITY

A hardware configuration program established into your computer's BIOS is the BIOS utility. At this stage, your computer must be configured and optimized and it is not necessary to run this utility. Nonetheless, you may need to run it if you encounter configuration issues. Press F2 to activate the BIOS utility.

Boot sequence

Activate the BIOS utility before setting the boot sequence in the BIOS utility. After that, choose Boot from the categories listed on the top of the screen.

Setting passwords

Activate the BIOS utility before setting a password on boot. After that, choose Security from the categories listed on the edge of the screen. To enable this feature, simply locate set supervisor password and insert a password. You may then enable or disable password on boot, but only when you have inserted a password for this feature. To properly save and exit the BIOS utility when you are through with making changes, simply select the F10 button.

POWER MANAGEMENT

The computer is also in possession of a built-in power management unit that monitors system activity. What is system activity? Well, it refers to any activity that involves one or more of the following devices; hard disk, mouse, keyboard, video memory, and peripherals connected to the computer. The computer stops some or even all of these devices if no activity is detected for some period. The main reason is to conserve energy.

Saving Power Disable Fast startup

Your computer can start quickly if it uses the Fast startup feature. That said, it checks for signals to start by using a small amount of power. Your computer's battery slowly drains by these checks. Turn off Fast startup if you want to reduce your computer's power requirements and environmental impact;

- Hit the Windows key button or choose the Windows start button
- After that, choose Settings > System > Power and sleep
- Choose Additional power settings
- Select what the power buttons do. Keep in mind that if you turn off Fast startup, then your computer will take

an extended period to start from sleep. Also, your computer will not start if it received an instruction to start over a network (Wake on LAN).

- Choose Change settings that are not available at the moment.

- Disable Turn on fast startup when you scroll down

- Finally, choose Save changes.

BATTERY PACK

The computer also has an embedded Lithium battery that enables you to use it for extended period.

Battery characteristics

Whenever you connect the computer to the AC adapter, the battery automatically recharges. Since your computer supports charge-in-use, it enables you to recharge the battery while you keep on operating the computer. Nonetheless, using the computer to recharge while it is tuned off significantly reduces charge time. When you travel or during a power failure, the battery will come in handy.

Charging the battery

Plug in the AC adapter to the laptop device, then connect to the power outlet.

Conditioning a new battery pack

There is a conditioning process that you should follow before you use a battery pack for the first time;

1. Plug in the AC adapter and ensure that the battery is fully charged
2. Put on the computer device and complete operating system
3. After that, disconnect the AC adapter
4. Also, use the battery power to operate the computer
5. Completely deplete the battery till the battery-low warning displays.
6. Before you fully charge the battery again, simply reconnect the AC adapter. Follow these steps again till the battery has been charged and discharged on three occasions.

For all new batteries, simply use this conditioning process. Also use this conditioning process on a battery that has not been used for an extended period.

The battery conditioning process will ensure that your battery approves of the maximum possible charge. You will not be able to obtain the maximum battery charge if you fail to follow this procedure, and it may lead to a shortened the battery's lifespan. That said, the following usage patterns adversely affect the useful lifespan of the battery;

- Making use of the computer on constant AC power
- Not recharging and discharging the battery to its extremes, as described above.
- Regular use. In other words, you will reach the end of its effective life as you use the battery. An embedded battery has a life span of more than a thousand charge/discharge cycles.

Optimizing battery life

You can get the most out of battery operation if you optimize the battery life. Besides, optimizing battery life prolongs the charge/recharge cycle and improves recharging efficiency. It is recommended to follow the suggestions set out below.

- Accessories that are not being used should be removed. These accessories include USB disk drive. The reason is that they keep on drawing power.
- Store your PC in a dry and cool place. The recommended temperature is 10 degree C or 50 degree F to 30 degree C or 86 degree F. The battery can self

discharge faster if the temperatures are higher. The battery life can be reduced if you recharge excessively.

- Closely monitor your battery and AC adapter

Checking the battery level

The power meter indicates the current battery level. On the taskbar, simply rest the cursor over the power or batty icon to see the battery's present charge level.

Battery Low warning

Pay attention to the power meter, especially when using battery power.

The recommended course of action depends on your situation when the battery-low warning appears; after the battery-low warning appears, simply connect the AC adapter immediately. If the battery is allowed to become completely depleted and it eventually shuts down, data may be lost.

1. Plug the AC adapter into the computer
2. After that, connect to the main power supply
3. Also, save all necessary or important files
4. Resume work. If you want to recharge the battery rapidly, then simply turn off the computer.

If the power outlet or AC adapter is not available;

1. Save all important or necessary files
2. Then, close all applications.
3. Finally, turn off the computer.

TRAVELLING WITH YOUR COMPUTER

You will get all the hints and tips you need when you are considering moving around or travelling with your computer device.

Disconnecting from the desktop

To disconnect your computer from external accessories, simply follow these steps below;

- Save any open files
- Get rid of discs from optical drive
- Put the device on a sleeping mode or do a complete shot down. You can also put it to hibernate mode.
- Close the display cover
- Disconnect the cord from the AC adapter.

- Disconnect the pointing device, keyboard, external monitor, printer, and other external devices.
- If you are using the Noble or Kensington lock to secure the computer, simply disconnect any of them.

Moving around

This simply indicates that you are only moving within short distances, for instance, from your bedroom to your kitchen.

Preparing the computer

Before you move the computer, simply close and latch the display cove to place it in sleep mode. Now, you can place the computer anywhere you go within the building. If you want to wake the computer from sleep mode, simply;

- Launch the display
- Then, touch and release the power button.

You may have to shut down the computer if you are taking the computer to a client's office or another building.

- Touch the Windows key
- Then, tap Power before selecting Shut Down.

Once you press the sleep hotkey or even close the display, you are directly putting the computer in sleep mode. Open the display, and press/release the power button when you are ready to use the computer again.

What to bring to meetings

Let us assume your meeting is relatively short, simply bring just your computer. But assuming your meeting is for an extended period and your battery is not fully charged, simply bring the AC adapter to plug in your computer in the meeting room. Reduce the drain on the battery if the meeting room does not have an electrical outlet. You can reduce the drain on the battery by putting it in sleep mode. Whenever you are not actively using the computer, simply press the sleep hotkey or close the display cover.

Taking the computer home

It simply indicates when you are taking your computer from your office to your home or vice versa.

Preparing the computer

Follow these steps to prepare the computer for the trip home, most especially after disconnecting the computer from your desktop;

- Make sure all media and compact discs are removed from the device. If you fail to remove the media, then you can cause damage to the drive head.
- Prevent the computer from sliding around and cushion it if it should fall by packing the computer in a protective case.

What you need to carry along; take these items with you;

- Power cord and AC adapter
- The printed setup guide.

Special considerations

To protect your computer while travelling to and from work, simply follow these guidelines;

- Keep the computer with you to minimize the effects of temperature changes.

- Leave the computer in the trunk of the car if you need to stop for a long period and cannot carry the computer with you. This can prevent the computer's exposure to excessive heat.

- Changes in humidity and temperature can result to condensation. Let the computer to go back to room temperature, and monitor the screen for condensation before turning on the computer. Allow the computer to come to room temperature slowly if the temperature change is greater than 10 degree C or 18 degree F. You can also decide to leave the computer in an environment with a temperature between outside and room temperature for 30 minutes.

Setting up a home office

You may choose to buy a second AC adapter if you constantly work on your computer at home. You can avoid carrying the additional weight to add from home if you own a second AC adapter. You might also want to include an external keyboard, mouse, or monitor if you use your computer at home for significant periods.

Ports and connectors

UNIVERSAL SERIAL BUS (USB)

A high-speed port that allows you to connect USB peripherals like the external keyboard, mouse, and additional storage (external hard disks), or other compatible devices is otherwise known as the USB port.

You can also use the USB port to charge devices like the smartphones, tablets, or other devices. When the computer is in hibernate or even turned off, some USB 3.0 ports support charging devices. In addition, you can connect multiple devices to just one USB port with the USB hub.

USB TYPE-C PORT A USB Type-C port is a connector that lets you to connect USB Type-C peripherals easily. These USB Type-C peripherals include the additional storage like an external drive or other compatible devices. Since the Type-C port can be reversed, connectors can be inserted with either side up.

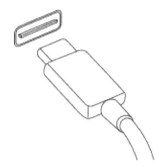

SD CARD READER UP; you can use the secure digital cards in a wide selection of digital tablets, cameras, media players, and cellular phones.

Inserting an SD Card

1. For the connector to point towards the port, simply align the card with the connectors facing down.

2. Then, carefully slide the card into the port. Try reconnecting the card slightly if you find you need to use any force to insert the card.

3. Push the card till it clicks into place. Some millimeters of the card will extend from beyond the slot. The Windows AutoPlay window may display if the card contains some files. It will also ask you if you intend to use a program to access the contents of the card.

SD, SDHC, and SDXC cards

While the different kinds of cards use the same overall design, it also covers different capacities. SD cards contain up to 4Gb, SDHC cards contain up to 32 GB, and SDXC cards contain up to 2048 GB (2 TB). The SDHC or SDXC compatible card readers are provided by your computer.

VIDEO AND AUDIO CONNECTORS

Use a video port to add an external monitor to your computer. The kind of port available depends on your computer's configuration.

- Make sure the computer is turned off and monitor power switch is also turned off.
- On the computer, simply attach the video cable to the monitor.
- Afterwards, connect the monitor power cable by plugging it into a properly grounded wall outlet.
- Follow the setup instructions in the monitor's user's guide.
- Turn on the monitor before the computer.
- The correct refresh rate and resolution should be detected automatically. Even though it is not

mandated, you can choose to change the display settings used by the computer.

Headphones and microphone

You can be allowed to connect audio devices if you have one or more 3.5 mm jacks on your computer. Plug in stereo headphones or powered speakers with your headphone port. The built-in speakers are usually disabled when you connect an audio device to the headphone. Also, connect an external microphone through the microphone port. Keep in mind that the built-in microphone is disabled when you connect a microphone.

HDMI

HDMI (High-Definition Multimedia interface) is a high-quality, digital video/audio interface. You can connect any compatible digital video/audio source like the set-top box, computer, DVD player, and video/audio receiver to any compatible digital video or audio monitor with your HDMI. A digital television is a good example of a compatible digital video or audio monitor. Even though the single cable ensures everything is tidy and neat, it also ensures that it offers easy connection and the best visual and audio quality.

- Insert the supervisor password and hit the Enter button to access the BIOS utility. A warning message appears when you insert the password incorrectly. Try again and hit the Enter button.
- A prompt appears at boot-up when the User password is set and the password on boot parameter is enabled.
- Insert the User password and hit the Enter button to use the computer. . A warning message appears when you insert the password incorrectly. Try again and hit the Enter button.

BIOS UTILITY

A hardware configuration program established into your computer's BIOS is the BIOS utility. At this stage, your computer must be configured and optimized and it is not necessary to run this utility. Nonetheless, you may need to run it if you encounter configuration issues. Press F2 to activate the BIOS utility.

Boot sequence

Activate the BIOS utility before setting the boot sequence in the BIOS utility. After that, choose Boot from the categories listed on the top of the screen.

Setting passwords

Activate the BIOS utility before setting a password on boot. After that, choose Security from the categories listed on the edge of the screen. To enable this feature, simply locate set supervisor password and insert a password. You may then enable or disable password on boot, but only when you have inserted a password for this feature. To properly save and exit the BIOS utility when you are through with making changes, simply select the F10 button.

POWER MANAGEMENT

The computer is also in possession of a built-in power management unit that monitors system activity. What is system activity? Well, it refers to any activity that involves one or more of the following devices; hard disk, mouse, keyboard, video memory, and peripherals connected to the computer. The computer stops some or even all of these devices if no activity is detected for some period. The main reason is to conserve energy.

Saving Power Disable Fast startup

Your computer can start quickly if it uses the Fast startup feature. That said, it checks for signals to start by using a small amount of power. Your computer's battery slowly drains by these checks. Turn off Fast startup if you want to reduce your computer's power requirements and environmental impact;

- Hit the Windows key button or choose the Windows start button
- After that, choose Settings > System > Power and sleep
- Choose Additional power settings
- Select what the power buttons do. Keep in mind that if you turn off Fast startup, then your computer will take

an extended period to start from sleep. Also, your computer will not start if it received an instruction to start over a network (Wake on LAN).

- Choose Change settings that are not available at the moment.

- Disable Turn on fast startup when you scroll down

- Finally, choose Save changes.

BATTERY PACK

The computer also has an embedded Lithium battery that enables you to use it for extended period.

Battery characteristics

Whenever you connect the computer to the AC adapter, the battery automatically recharges. Since your computer supports charge-in-use, it enables you to recharge the battery while you keep on operating the computer. Nonetheless, using the computer to recharge while it is tuned off significantly reduces charge time. When you travel or during a power failure, the battery will come in handy.

Charging the battery

Plug in the AC adapter to the laptop device, then connect to the power outlet.

Conditioning a new battery pack

There is a conditioning process that you should follow before you use a battery pack for the first time;

- Plug in the AC adapter and ensure that the battery is fully charged
- Put on the computer device and complete operating system
- After that, disconnect the AC adapter
- Also, use the battery power to operate the computer
- Completely deplete the battery till the battery-low warning displays.
- Before you fully charge the battery again, simply reconnect the AC adapter. Follow these steps again till the battery has been charged and discharged on three occasions.

For all new batteries, simply use this conditioning process. Also use this conditioning process on a battery that has not been used for an extended period.

The battery conditioning process will ensure that your battery approves of the maximum possible charge. You will not be able to obtain the maximum battery charge if you fail to follow this procedure, and it may lead to a cut in the battery's lifespan. That said, the following usage patterns adversely affect the useful lifespan of the battery;

- Making use of the computer on constant AC power

- Not recharging and discharging the battery to its extremes, as described above.
- Regular use. In other words, you will reach the end of its effective life as you use the battery. An embedded battery has a life span of more than a thousand charge/discharge cycles.

Optimizing battery life

You can get the most out of battery operation if you optimize the battery life. Besides, optimizing battery life prolongs the charge/recharge cycle and improves recharging efficiency. It is recommended to follow the suggestions set out below.

- Accessories that are not being used should be removed. These accessories include USB disk drive. The reason is that they keep on drawing power.
- Store your PC in a dry and cool place. The recommended temperature is 10 degree C or 50 degree F to 30 degree C or 86 degree F. The battery can self discharge faster if the temperatures are higher. The battery life can be reduced if you recharge excessively.
- Closely monitor your battery and AC adapter

Checking the battery level

The power meter indicates the current battery level. On the taskbar, simply rest the cursor over the power or batty icon to see the battery's present charge level.

Battery Low warning

Pay attention to the power meter, especially when using battery power.

The recommended course of action depends on your situation when the battery-low warning appears; after the battery-low warning appears, simply connect the AC adapter immediately. If the battery is allowed to become completely depleted and it eventually shuts down, data may be lost.

- Plug the AC adapter into the computer
- After that, connect to the main power supply
- Also, save all necessary or important files
- Resume work. If you want to recharge the battery rapidly, then simply turn off the computer.

The power outlet or AC adapter is not available?

- Save all important or necessary files
- Then, close all applications.
- Finally, turn off the computer.

TRAVELLING WITH YOUR COMPUTER

With this section, you can access hints and tips to consider when you are using your computer to move around or travel.

Disconnecting from the desktop

To disconnect your computer from external accessories, simply follow these steps below;

- Save any open files
- Get rid of discs from optical drive
- Put the device on a sleeping mode or do a complete shot down. You can also put it to hibernate mode.
- Close the display cover
- Disconnect the cord from the AC adapter.
- Disconnect the pointing device, keyboard, external monitor, printer, and other external devices.
- If you are using the Noble or Kensington lock to secure the computer, simply disconnect any of them.

Moving around

This simply indicates that you are only moving within short distances, for instance, from your bedroom to your kitchen.